"Turns upside down everything marriage counselors have advised in magazines, talk shows and bestsellers for the last decade."
—*USA Today*

♡

Relationship Professionals Agree: *The Dirty Half Dozen* Rewrites the Book of Love!

♡

"The most important book on relationships this year. If you are unhappy with the one you love, this little book can change your life and relationship. I recommend it to all my patients."
—**Steven Frank, Ph.D., Clinical Psychologist, North Detroit General Hospital**

♡

"A witty, humorous, direct, effective, and readable way to get closer to loved ones. Read this book."
—**Howard Burman, Ph.D., Professor and Chair, Communications Department, California State University**

♡

"A provocative and insightful guide that will improve the quality of your intimate relationships. Follow Dr. Nagler's rules, they work."
—**R. Douglas Peters, Ph.D., Professor of Psychology, Jacksonville State Univerity**

THE DIRTY HALF DOZEN

Six Radical Rules to Make Relationships Last

by **William Nagler, M.D.,**
and **Anne Androff**

WARNER BOOKS

A Time Warner Company

Warner Books, Inc. 1271 Avenue of the Americas, New York, NY 10020

W A Time Warner Company

Printed in the United States of America
First trade printing: August 1992
10 9 8 7 6 5 4 3 2

Library of Congress Cataloging-in-Publication Data
Nagler, William.
    The dirty half dozen : six radical rules to make relationships
last / William Nagler and Anne Androff.
      p.   cm.
    ISBN 0-446-39408-4
    1. Interpersonal relationships. 2. Interpersonal communication.
I. Androff. Anne, II Title.
    HM132.N32   1991
158'2—dc20   90-50527
                                           CIP

Book design by Giorgetta Bell McRee
Cover design and illustration by Corsillo/Manzone

*Dedicated to the memory of J.V.M.,
who taught me how to think.*

CONTENTS

INTRODUCTION

Lisa was a successful broker who was intelligent, caring, and very sexy. I was a psychiatrist who was deeply committed to our relationship. We talked openly and honestly about everything. We shared every day. We worked at keeping our relationship alive.

Lisa and I lived together for almost five years. But it ended in hell, or as close to hell as I'd come in thirty-five years. At the end, we didn't talk, we just screamed. We didn't reason, we just raved. And we didn't make love, we just had sex, and neither of us enjoyed it.

We started to have problems about a year into our relationship, when we both began to lose interest in having sex quite so often. The fireworks had started to fade. Assuming that the problem might run deep, we sought professional help.

Our therapist encouraged us to discuss everything with each other. So we began to air all of our feelings openly and honestly, and we strived to put the "romance" back in our lives. We scheduled romantic weekends at rustic inns. We took breaks in the middle of the day to come home and make love. We followed all the traditional rules for intimacy and open, honest communication. And yet things got worse. The more we tried to be close, the further apart we drifted. We didn't know it then, but we were working our relationship to death.

This book began five years ago with the disintegration of my relationship with Lisa. I felt a need to make some sense of what had happened, and I wanted to discover why trying to make things better by using the traditional tricks of my psychiatric trade had led to so much hate, anger, and heartbreak. I needed to know why doing everything I had been taught to do to keep us together had failed.

I began to look for patterns in my patients. Tami and Scott had come to me because they were having fierce arguments on a regular basis. They were deeply in love, and they wanted to stop fighting, because they knew it would bring them closer together. So I taught them how to communicate openly and honestly with each other. A year later they filed for divorce.

Judy and Billy sought my help because they were having problems with money. I taught them how to share and compromise, and sent them on their way. Their relationship ended in six months.

My files were full of people I had driven apart, by teaching them what I had been taught would bring them closer together. Clearly, something was wrong.

Then I met a patient who changed the way I practiced psychiatry. Terri had been happily married for eight years, but she had just had a short-lived affair with a man she met through mutual friends. Her lover was a glamorous fashion designer, very romantic, attentive, and exciting to a slightly bored housewife with a busy husband and two small children. But after a few afternoons with her new lover, Terri realized that he was not what she wanted. She wanted her husband and family, and she swiftly ended the affair.

Terri was consumed with guilt and humiliation. She wanted to confess everything to her husband, to cleanse her soul and bring them closer. I started to encourage her to do so, because this was the open and honest thing to do. But as I looked more closely at her problem, I had a second thought. Terri and her husband weren't apart. In fact, they got along fine. Their relationship was terrific. Terri's affair had been a spur-of-the-moment, thoughtless act, not the result of a troubled relationship. So, what would be the point of confession? What would a confession do to Terri's relationship with her husband? It would break it, I thought. Her husband would be hurt and angry, and possibly vengeful and unforgiving. It occurred to me at that moment that total honesty was exactly what was *not* called for.

So I said to Terri, "You told me all about what happened. And that's fine. But, don't tell your husband." There was a long pause, during which Terri looked at me as if I were a visitor from another planet. I broke it. "Why do you think I don't want you to tell him?" I asked her. No response. Another pause. "What effect do you think cleansing your soul will have on your husband? What do you think this disclosure will do to your relationship? You're getting along fine now, as it is," I said. "You had an affair, you ended it, and now you know what's important to you." Another pause. "Keep your mouth shut, and get on with your life." She did, her relationship survived, and I knew I was on to something.

From that moment on, I began my quest to find out why trying to fix my own and other people's relationships had actually driven people apart. For the first time in my career, I focused *inter*personally, instead of in*tra*personally—I looked at what was going on between people, instead of inside them. I took a look at open, honest communication, to see what it really did to relationships. I dug deep into the psychiatric literature to see what studies and research had been done about repairing relationships, and why repair almost always made things worse.

By surveying more than thirty years of psychiatric literature, and submitting over a thousand studies on successful and unsuccessful relationships to a computerized factor analysis, I found something curious: **There were six universal behavior patterns that were always present in relationships that fell apart.** And these were the exact behaviors that I and other psychiatrists had been *teaching* people for years. We had been advising people to work on keeping romance alive, to fight fair, to talk out their problems, to always tell the truth, to make reasonable compromises about money, and to ignore the little things that bugged them in their relationships. But by doing so we were inadvertently undermining the relationships we had been trying to save. Our advice tended to create tension and stress that weren't there before.

After analyzing the data on couples who had followed conventional psychiatric advice (and consequently failed in relationships), I took a look at couples who didn't follow conventional advice, and I made an even more startling discovery: **People in relationships who were *not* completely open and honest about everything got along better than people in relationships who told the truth.** I found that "dishonest" people in relationships tended to be much happier, and stayed together longer. It became clear to me that, contrary to what I had been taught and what I believed, satisfying long-term relationships were *not* about love, passion, trust, romance, honesty, or intimacy. Successful relationships were about simply getting along. Good relationships were not about total communication and openness. Good relationships were about being comfortable together.

I realized that it was the expectation of perpetual fireworks that had started the problems for Lisa and me. Our expectations of passion forever had done us in. In retrospect, I see that it was working on our relationship, working to keep romance alive, that had finished us off. We weren't as passionate about each other as we had been at the start of our relationship, but that should have been expected. Fireworks can't last forever; they're not supposed to. But being comfortable together can. We had been comfortable, and we should have left things at that. Working on our relationship, talking everything out, had made us uptight and hostile, and bringing our relationship into therapy had finished us off. Artificially creating romance and situations to be together didn't do a thing but create tension and drive us apart.

I remembered Judy and Billy, my patients who had the

money problems. I had tried to improve their relationship by teaching them to share and compromise, and things had gotten worse. The tension of negotiating every transaction drove them apart. It would have been far better for me to have told them to open up separate bank accounts and to divide their financial responsibilities down the middle. They would probably still be together today.

So in my own relationships and in counseling others, I took a new approach. I stopped focusing on intimacy, openness, honesty, and total communication. I concentrated instead on what makes people get along: **The ability to feel relaxed together.**

I began teaching my patients *not* to strive to keep romance alive, *not* to talk about everything, and *not* to always tell the truth. I encouraged people with relationship problems *not* to fight fair, *not* to make compromises about money, and not to worry about what they assumed was important in their relationships. While what I did may sound radical, essentially all I was advising them to do was to behave in ways that would reduce tension between them. I encouraged my patients to look at their relationships realistically, rather than idealistically, to recognize that perfect relationships don't exist, but that happy, lasting relationships can in tension-free environments. I showed them that my offbeat rules for lasting relationships were the key to reducing the tension that had led to their problems. And as they began to apply the rules to their lives, I saw their relationships improve.

This book is about the behaviors that I discovered facilitate tension reduction and help people get along. It summarizes in six truths my five years of experience and research into what makes relationships work. I view these truths as *rules* for successful relationships because they are the most significant facilitators of happiness and relationship success that I have found. The rules work by helping couples reduce tension in such key areas of potential relationship trouble as intimacy, honesty, communication, conflict, and money.

At first glance, the rules in this book may seem like cruel tricks to play on your partner, an attempt to deceive and hoodwink him or her into getting along with you. *The Dirty Half Dozen*, however, is not a book of dirty tricks that can help a bankrupt relationship survive, but a revelatory new way of helping people recognize and foster the qualities in relationships that really matter. Abstract concepts like "romance" and "truth" are simply that. This book dares to show you what they mean in the real-life world of relationships. How do you think the truth will make your partner feel, I always ask. What effect do you think telling the truth will have on your relationship? What is more important, the truth or the survival of a relationship? Do you want to fight fair or look forward to going home to someone at night? Do you want an "honest" relationship, or a relationship that is satisfying, makes you happy, and will last? The truth is that happy couples don't try to entertain each other, they relax and enjoy each other's company. They don't fight fair, they pick their battles carefully. They don't talk about everything. They aren't obsessed with the truth. They know that total honesty requires infinite tact. They don't compromise about money. Successful couples control it. And people in good relationships don't worry about what they think is important. Happy couples pay selective attention to the little things going on between them.

The rules are not a means of improving your relationship through radical change, they are a means of making your relationship more satisfying and lasting by letting it be.

William Nagler, M.D.
June 1990

AUTHOR'S NOTE

For the sake of clarity and accessibility, this book is written as a series of statements of truths about relationships. My concepts are presented simply, so that you can easily apply them to your relationship today.

THE DIRTY HALF DOZEN

▲

Rule One:
DON'T KEEP THE ROMANCE ALIVE.

▲

Rule Two:
DON'T FIGHT FAIR.

▲

Rule Three:
DON'T TALK ABOUT EVERYTHING.

▲

Rule Four:
DON'T ALWAYS TELL THE TRUTH.

▲

Rule Five:
DON'T LET GO OF THE MONEY.

▲

Rule Six:
DON'T WORRY ABOUT WHAT YOU
THINK IS IMPORTANT.

Rule One:

DON'T KEEP THE ROMANCE ALIVE.

Don't keep the romance alive.

You can't, you never could, and you'll never be able to.

So stop trying.

You don't want to.

The best way to destroy a relationship, any relationship, is to try to keep the romance alive.

You can't bring the excitement back, once it starts to fade.

Working on making a relationship exciting is guaranteed to destroy whatever spark may be left.

PASSION FADES

The spark of romance, passion, and excitement that kindles most relationships fades over time.

Passion must fade, so you can get on with your life.

Passion must fade, so you can focus your energy and attention on other important aspects of life, like earning a living and raising your children.

Sexual passion fades over time.

Intellectual passion fades over time.

Vocational passion fades over time, too.

Most relationships, sexual and otherwise, lose their burning passion as time passes.

The spark remains, but the heat must fade.

EXCITEMENT DIES

There's nothing you can do to prevent the excitement in your relationship from dying, either.

So stop trying.

By trying to keep the spark and excitement in a relationship alive, you are hastening its demise.

Ride the horse in the direction it's going.

Let go.

Let romance fade.

Let passion die.

Let excitement go.

Passion will burn itself out over time, no matter what you do.

So let it go.

STOP ENTERTAINING

You can't constantly entertain, please, and enchant your partner.

You cannot make your relationship constantly exciting.

It cannot be done.

In fact, trying to is destructive.

You run out of material.

Think about it.

Most of us have a limited amount of new material in our heads.

We have a limited number of new things to say, funny comments to make, and novel things to do.

After a while, your partner has seen it all, and heard it all.

After a while, you deplete your supply of new material.

THE KEY

Tension reduction is the key to long-term relationships.

Tension reduction is the most common characteristic of successful long-term relationships.

Tension reduction is the most important thing you can do to make your relationship last, and to make it better.

Let romance run its course, so you can get on with your life.

Successful relationships are not based on passion, excitement, or romance.

Successful relationships are based on tension reduction.

CONDITION EACH OTHER
TO RELAX

Successful relationships result from people being relaxed and comfortable with each other.

Happy couples have conditioned each other to relax.

Happy couples have learned how to be together without having to do anything at all.

Good relationships are not about exciting activities.

Good relationships are about people being in the same room at the same time and being comfortable without doing anything.

Good relationships are about just being together.

Stop trying to entertain your partner.

Stop trying to make your relationship fun and exciting.

Let your partner, and those around you, relax.

Condition those around you to let things be.

UNHAPPY COUPLES

Unhappy couples are tension arousers.

Unhappy couples have become accustomed to being tense.

Unhappy couples are always looking for something exciting to do, which raises their level of tension, and makes them more unhappy.

Happiness in relationships is not about stimulation and excitement.

Happiness is about just being together.

And not having to do anything at all.

Just being together.

STOP

Stop trying to make your relationship entertaining.

Stop trying to make things fun and exciting.

You can't.

Stop trying.

Relax.

WHEN YOU WERE A CHILD

When you were a child, your happiest times were when your parents gave you the freedom to play and be yourself.

You were happy, and there was nothing special you had to do.

You could just be there, with your parents, and be yourself.

You were there, and they were there, free and at ease.

There was no tension, stress, anxiety, or expectation.

There was nothing any of you had to do.

You could just be you, there with them, without doing anything at all.

Do the same for your relationship.

WHAT ABOUT LOVE AND SEX?

Sex and love have nothing to do with successful long-term relationships.

Sex is fun.

And love is a terrific feeling.

Having sex with someone you love, or being in love with someone you have sex with, can be wonderful.

But sex and love are tension arousers.

They create feelings of passion and excitement.

And passion and excitement increase tension.

Enjoy sex and feelings of love while you have them.

But don't assume your relationship is dead when they fade, as they inevitably will.

And don't try to rekindle passion and excitement.

Trying to keep romance alive has the opposite effect.

Enjoy the spark of sex and love while you can.

Enjoy your passion and excitement while you've got it.

Treasure the memory, and get on with your life.

SEPARATE SEX AND LOVE

Love has nothing to do with sex.

And sex has nothing to do with love.

Separating sex and love in your mind will help your relationship survive.

You can be sexually attracted to someone you do not want to have a relationship with.

Most of us have experienced some degree of sexual attraction, at one time or another, to a person whom we did not particularly like.

You can also be madly in love with someone who does not interest you sexually, and with whom you do not want to have a relationship.

Most of us have also fallen in love, at one time or another, with someone for whom we experienced little or no sexual desire.

Neither sex nor love are essential to long-term relationship survival.

WHAT IS SEX?

Sex is a particular kind of attraction between two people, a biochemical attraction, based on compatible and raging levels of hormones.

Sexual desire is animal, hormonal, and glandular.

Over time, when you don't sleep, you get tired.

Over time, when you don't eat, you get hungry.

Over time, when you don't have sex, you get horny.

Your sex drive is a natural and healthy part of being alive, an automatic biochemical process, that builds up over time.

The intensity of your excitement about your partner will fade over time, however.

It's inevitable.

And there's nothing you can do to bring it back.

So don't try.

WHAT IS LOVE?

Love is an attraction, too.

Love is a particular type of personality attraction, based on like values, compatible backgrounds, and common behavior patterns.

Love is emotional, behavioral, and nonsexual.

Love is a state of attraction to another person, a feeling of tension arousal.

The arousal that we call love must also naturally fade over time.

It has to.

And like sexual arousal, there's nothing you can do to bring it back.

So don't try.

LET PASSION RUN ITS COURSE

Passion runs its course, and sex and love fade over time.

Your partner can't continue to excite you the same way forever.

And there's nothing you can do about it.

So stop trying.

DON'T FIGHT FAIR.

Don't fight fair.

You don't want to.

A fair fight is one in which both participants are equally equipped and prepared to do battle.

The participants in fair fights play by the rules of battle.

Don't do either.

"Fighting fair" is considered to be productive by most relationship counselors.

But they're wrong.

The trouble with "fighting fair" is that you have a winner and a loser.

Both are bad for long-term relationships.

So don't fight fair.

Fight dirty.

Don't get into the ring.

Don't even bother to put your gloves on.

Give up before you fight.

Give in.

You'll get what you want this way.

A lasting relationship.

GIVE UP

Give up.

Most things in your relationship are not really worth fighting about.

Think about it.

You *can* avoid any fight.

Don't bother to get into it.

It's not worth it.

Think about it.

Only one of you has to remember to play dirty by not getting into the fight.

It only takes one of you to back down.

Just one of you has to step back and get out of the way, so there's no one left to fight with.

Don't fight fair.

Don't even bother to fight.

Give up.

Give in.

On purpose.

IS THIS REALLY WORTH FIGHTING FOR?

You can avoid ninety percent of all battles in your relationships, if you simply take a moment to ask yourself, "Is this really worth fighting for?"

If the answer is yes, ask yourself again.

Most things in your relationship just don't matter that much.

Most things in your relationship are not that vitally important.

Most things in your relationship are not worth fighting for.

Pick your battles carefully.

Win in your relationship.

Lose the skirmishes.

Choose not to fight.

TUNNEL VISION

Avoiding battles, like fostering successful relationships, is largely a matter of tunnel vision.

You see what you look for.

Don't go looking for fights.

Look for ways out of them.

There's always an escape hatch in verbal battle.

There's always a loophole you can find to slip your way out of a fight.

Keep your sense of humor, too.

Your sense of humor is your most powerful weapon for defusing conflicts and avoiding battles.

When things heat up, crack a joke.

Say something silly.

Do something dumb.

Just get out of the situation.

IF BATTLE IS INEVITABLE

If battle is inevitable, if you have to get into it, remember:

Keep your battles short and to the point.

Keep your relationship from becoming a casualty.

Fight about what you're fighting about.

You've got to be specific to protect your relationship.

Fight only about whatever it is that you are in disagreement about.

Stay focused on the conflict at hand.

Completely.

EAT FIRST

It helps to eat.

You can avoid a lot of relationship conflicts if you both have had something to eat first.

Half the time, having a full stomach will prevent major fights.

Blood-sugar battles are often what you are really fighting.

When your blood sugar is low, you are cranky and out of control.

When your blood sugar is low, things that normally wouldn't bother you seem like major events.

Eating something, anything, raises your blood sugar and your ability to cope.

Eat something first, anything, and see what happens.

No fighting before breakfast, because your blood sugar is low.

No fighting before lunch, for the same reason.

And the same goes for before dinner, too.

YOU ARE VULNERABLE

You are particularly vulnerable at times of the day when your blood sugar is low.

You are out of control, and you don't know it, because low blood sugar causes epinephrine release.

And epinephrine release makes your temper short, your anger high, and rational thinking very difficult.

So don't fight unless you've both had something to eat first.

Most of the time, after you eat something, at least one of you will be able to remember not to fight.

Most of the time, after you eat something, at least one of you will be able to step back and ask the all-important question:

"Is this really worth fighting for?"

The answer is usually no.

SLEEP

Make sure you both get enough sleep, too.

More than fifty percent of all urban Americans suffer from mild to moderate sleep deprivation today.

And it's showing up in their relationships.

Sleep deprivation also causes epinephrine release, which causes the same craziness as low blood sugar.

When people don't get enough sleep, they become angry, irritable, and irrational, just as when blood sugar is low.

Battles can be avoided, if just one of you is awake enough to remember not to fight.

It's hard not to fight when you're tired.

You can't think clearly when you're tired.

You can't function fully and you can't make rational decisions.

What you can do when you're tired is get irritable and fight.

Rest before, to avoid battle.

Sleep is the greatest tension reducer in the world.

You need sleep to be a human being.

You need sleep to behave like a human being.

Sleep on it.

Inevitable conflicts often go away by morning.

THE WRONG PLACE
AT THE WRONG TIME

A lot of fights happen because you are in the wrong place at the wrong time, too.

After a bad day at the office, your partner comes home and takes it all out on you.

The fight has nothing to do with you, or anything you've done.

The fight is a result of your being in the wrong place at the wrong time.

You're the recipient of your partner's pent-up anger and frustration.

About something else.

You're an unfortunate and abused sounding board, just because you're available.

The battle really isn't about what you are fighting about.

The battle is about your partner being angry and frustrated, about other things.

Get out of there.

Rule Three:

DON'T TALK ABOUT EVERYTHING.

Don't talk about everything.

We live in a zestfully overcommunicative age.

We are supposed to talk everything out, work everything out, and resolve everything.

Don't.

Talking things out often doesn't work.

Talking things out often doesn't help.

The *worst* thing you can do with some problems is to talk about them.

If you and your partner disagree on something like abortion, for example, all the discussion in the world is not likely to resolve anything between you.

Talking about the situation will just heighten your differences.

And increase tension.

Find out what your partner's position is, if you are curious, and then drop it.

You don't have to discuss everything.

HOLD OFF

Don't discuss things for a change.

Wait a while, wait a week.

Don't talk things out right away, if ever.

Stand off a while.

Let things be.

Things change and settle over time.

That's the time to talk, if ever.

RIGHT NOW?

Ask your partner, "Do we really have to talk about this, right now?"

"Really?"

"Do we?"

"Right now?"

"Are you sure?"

The answer is probably that now is not necessarily the time.

So don't.

You'll get along better.

Talking about a lot of things makes them worse, because a lot of things can't be resolved, and talking about them only increases tension between you and your partner.

You really don't have to discuss everything.

You are better off not discussing some things to death.

Stay away if you can from politics, morality, and religion.

Clarify your partner's position and beliefs if you are curious.

But don't have major discussions.

You can't and won't agree on everything with your partner.

And the more you discuss deeply held moral, political, and religious beliefs and values, the more tension you create.

Don't talk your relationship to death.

DON'T LET IT ALL HANG OUT

Letting it all hang out, or talking about everything in totally open, honest, and forthright terms, usually makes matters worse.

Most of the things that you think you have to talk about, you don't.

Think about it.

You don't discuss everything with other people.

You don't have to discuss everything with other people.

You will always disagree about some things.

Some things are best left unsaid, and undiscussed.

Your partner is better off not knowing some things.

TIME OUT

You also need time to be alone.

You need time out, to be yourself, to be by yourself.

You need time to let off steam, alone.

You need your own space, territory, and solitude.

You need some private time for yourself.

So does your partner.

Give your partner the freedom to be alone.

Allow yourself the pleasure of solitude.

It's good for both of you.

DON'T TRY SO HARD

Stop trying so hard.

The worst thing you can do to your relationship is to try too hard to work things out.

Stop trying so hard to make things better.

Stop trying.

Don't make an effort at all.

Let things be.

You are much more attractive to others, and more pleasant to be with, when you are not trying too hard.

You come across far better when you are not trying to impress or please others or to insinuate yourself.

Why?

Because you are decreasing tension, simply by letting things be.

STOP TRYING TO PLEASE

Stop trying to please, impress, or improve your partner.

You are much easier to get along with when you're not up to something.

We all are.

Hundreds of people have literally worked their relationships into the ground, while trying to improve them.

You now know why.

So don't.

BEGINNINGS AND ENDINGS

Beginnings and endings are the most important times of the day for your relationship.

Because beginnings and endings are the times when you are most likely to make an effort.

Don't.

Lighten up.

Take time to renew your relationship.

Take time to start well, to end well.

Don't fight.

Don't complain.

Don't criticize.

Don't do anything at all at the beginning and ending of the day.

NO NEGATIVES

Avoid negatives during the early-morning and late-evening hours of the day.

Avoid negatives when you see each other at the end of your workday.

Set a positive tone for your time together.

Take time to renew your relationship.

Take time to befriend each other, again.

Be friendly.

Compliment.

Praise.

Be considerate.

Make small talk.

Pass the moments well.

IMPORTANT MOMENTS

The most important moments of your relationship are at the beginning and ending of things.

Take time for tension reduction at these moments.

Take this time to set the tone for your time together.

Withhold criticism.

Don't try to improve, change, or help.

A FIRST DATE

You don't start out a successful first date, a successful first meeting, or a successful first anything by criticizing, complaining, or trying to improve another person.

Life doesn't work like that.

Relationships don't work like that, either.

Successful relationships start well and end well.

Every day.

Set aside time for good beginnings and endings.

Don't make your beginnings and endings anything special.

Don't make them anything at all.

Make them a time of tension reduction.

Rule Four:

DON'T ALWAYS TELL THE TRUTH.

Don't always tell the truth.

Learn to lie.

Truth requires total honesty.

Total honesty requires infinite tact.

Both are impossible.

Neither exists.

Lie a little.

Your partner doesn't really want, need, or care to know exactly how you feel and precisely what you are thinking.

DECREASE TENSION

You can't decrease tension by being totally honest.

Total honesty flies in the face of common sense.

Honesty isn't realistic.

The truth makes people feel bad.

Decrease tension.

Hide the truth.

Cover up.

"Am I gaining weight?"

"You look wonderful to me."

Don't tell the truth; it would only make your partner feel bad.

"Am I looking older?"

"You look beautiful."

Finesse around honesty, to preserve your relationship.

"Do I look like hell or what?"

"You look like 'what'; you look just fine."

Tactfully get out of there.

YOU DON'T WANT CRITICISM

You don't want or like criticism.

Neither does your partner.

Your partner doesn't really need to see or hear the truth about everything.

Many truths are best left undiscussed, unsaid, and untalked about.

The truth often hurts and makes things worse.

Your partner doesn't want to know the truth, doesn't need or care to.

OTHER PEOPLE DON'T CARE

Leave out your reasons "why," as well.

Other people don't really care why you did what you did, or why you didn't.

"Why" doesn't matter.

Reasons "why" do not decrease tension, or make other people feel good about themselves.

Reasons "why" are useless justifications.

Stop justifying.

Other people do not need your explanations as much as you think they do.

DON'T ASK "WHY?" QUESTIONS

Don't ask "Why?" questions of people, either.

People don't know "why."

People don't care to know "why," either.

"Why?" questions only make other people feel bad.

You can't answer a "Why?" question without feeling bad about yourself.

"Why?" questions are discriminatory.

"Why?" questions require evaluation.

Nobody likes to be evaluated.

"Why did you do this?"

"Why did you do that?"

You don't know.

So don't ask.

ASK "WHAT?" QUESTIONS

Ask "What?" questions.

"What?" questions are easy.

You can answer a "What?" question.

"What?" questions don't make people feel bad.

"What happened?"

"What's going on here?"

"What?" questions require a factual statement of reality, a report of what's going on.

"What?" questions require a description.

Not an evaluation.

BECAUSE I'M A HORRIBLE HUMAN BEING

The answer to most "Why?" questions is usually some variation of "Because I'm a horrible human being, a failure as a person, and I deserve to be shot."

"What?" questions are different.

The answer to most "What?" questions is usually some variation of "Well, this happened, and this happened, and this happened. Okay?"

"Why?" questions make people feel bad.

"What?" questions make people feel good.

"Why?" questions stop communication.

"What?" questions keep things going.

"Why?" questions raise anxiety.

"What?" questions decrease tension.

EVALUATIVE STATEMENTS

Evaluative statements like "That's good," "That's bad," or "That's stupid" block communication and raise tension.

Evaluative statements contain adjectives that make people feel bad.

Evaluative statements have no place in your relationship vocabulary.

People can't deal with evaluations.

You don't like them.

Nobody does.

Nobody likes being evaluated.

Evaluations and evaluative statements are counterproductive tension producers.

DESCRIPTIVE STATEMENTS

You can hear a descriptive statement from another person without going off the deep end.

Descriptive statements facilitate communication.

Descriptive statements like "That makes me feel good," "That makes me feel bad," or "That makes me feel stupid" are fine.

Descriptive statements contain adverbs and adjectives.

You can listen to, feel, and experience a descriptive statement without feeling bad.

So can other people.

Descriptive statements create a neutral, tension-free environment to exchange information in.

Descriptive statements keep conversation and communication going, by decreasing tension.

HOW TO ASK QUESTIONS

Ask "What?" questions, not "Why?" questions.

"What happened that made you late?"

"The car broke down."

"Why are you late?"

"Because I'm a horrible human being, a failure as a person, and I deserve to be shot."

One question requires a neutral description of reality.

The other question requires a judgmental evaluation.

"What happened that the cap is off the toothpaste tube?"

"I forgot to put it back on. Sorry."

Fine.

"Why is the cap off the toothpaste tube?"

"Because I'm a horrible human being, a failure as a person, and I deserve to be shot."

Disaster.

FEEL GOOD OR FEEL BAD

"What?" questions make other people feel good, by eliciting information and decreasing tension.

"Why?" questions make other people feel bad, by being judgmental and raising anxiety.

The difference between "What?" questions and "Why?" questions, in the long run, is nondiscriminatory tension-reducing communication and long-term relationships.

DESCRIBE, DON'T EVALUATE FEELINGS

When you describe your feelings, instead of evaluating them, you are also facilitating tension reduction.

When you evaluate your feelings, you are making yourself and other people feel bad.

Feel the difference between:

"That makes me feel bad."

And:

"That's bad."

One statement facilitates communication and decreases tension, by describing the way you feel.

The other statement blocks communication, by making a value judgment.

When you describe your feelings, you are answering "What?" questions.

You are giving people information.

When you evaluate your feelings, you are answering "Why?" questions.

"Why?" questions make people feel bad.

Make people feel good, instead.

UNHAPPY COUPLES

Unhappy couples work on their relationships by asking "Why?" questions, and create tension.

Happy couples ask "What?" questions, get a description of reality, and decrease tension.

Unhappy couples worry about how they are doing and "Why?" they are doing it.

Happy couples ask "What?" and get on with things.

The difference between tension-reducing and tension-producing relationships is the use of descriptive instead of evaluative communication.

Rule Five:

DON'T LET GO OF THE MONEY.

The person who controls the money in a relationship, controls the power in the relationship.

Don't let go of the money in your relationship.

Think about it.

The power in a relationship lies in the control of the money.

Whoever controls the money, controls the relationship.

Power lies with control of how money is spent.

HALF OF ALL RELATIONSHIP PROBLEMS

Half of all relationship problems have to do with money.

Money may not be everything.

But money is a major source of tension and conflict in relationships.

Money is also a major force in successful long-term relationship survival.

Use money right.

Don't let go of the power and the control of your relationship.

Control the money.

Keep the power.

For yourself.

Both of you.

MAKE THINGS EQUAL

You can't control equal earning.

But you can control equal spending.

Put half of the money that comes into your relationship in one bank account.

Put the other half of the money that comes into your relationship in another bank account.

Set up two bank accounts, and put all money into both, equally.

Make expenses come out of both accounts equally.

You have total control over your account.

Your partner has total control over his or her account.

Mutually agreed on basic living expenses come out of both accounts, equally.

The rest is up to each of you.

HOW TO SPEND MONEY

Spend your half of the money, exactly how you want to spend it.

Your partner does the same.

After basic living expenses, which are split fifty-fifty, the rest of the money is controlled by both of you.

Separately, equally, and totally.

You both keep power this way.

There's no such thing as win-win when it comes to money or monetary compromises in relationships.

Don't compromise your power.

Don't compromise about money.

Control money completely.

Both of you.

Rule Six:

DON'T WORRY ABOUT WHAT YOU THINK IS IMPORTANT.

Worry.

You need to worry more.

But don't worry about what you think is important.

Don't worry about money problems, illness in the family, or unemployment.

Don't worry about your sex life, how happy you are in your relationship, or the quality of intimacy you experience with your partner.

Don't worry about whether you've actually got what you want: a Cinderella and the Prince relationship, television and the movies' total, fulfilling, perfect relationship.

Worry about the little things.

Because it's the little things that destroy relationships over time.

You will make it through dire catastrophes, major disasters, and death.

But the little things will do you in, eventually.

If you let them.

It's the small stuff that brings most relationships to ruin.

UNATTENDED LITTLE THINGS

It's the unattended little things, over time, that increase tension and destroy relationships.

Start paying attention to the small stuff.

Because the small stuff becomes the big stuff.

You will survive major calamity, disaster, and death.

You will not survive the top off the toothpaste tube, on a daily basis.

The toilet seat left up, often enough, can kill you.

That pile of clothes on the floor can be fatal.

The little things are everything in terms of tension reduction.

The casual details of everyday life are what allow long-term relationships to survive.

YOU CANNOT SURVIVE

You cannot survive inattention to the little things that drive your partner crazy.

The little things drive you crazy, too.

It's the little things that destroy relationships, by building tension.

Start paying attention to the tiny details of everyday life.

The small stuff and the way that you handle it will determine how long your relationship survives.

Make an effort.

Accommodate your partner's little demands.

Pay attention to his or her small requests.

Pay attention to the small stuff.

GOOD STUFF, TOO

Pay attention to good little stuff, too.

Try an unexpected kiss on the cheek.

A "My, you look nice today."

Pay an uncalled-for compliment.

Partners in successful relationships make their partners feel good about themselves, by emphasizing the small stuff.

Pay attention.

Say something nice about something that doesn't matter.

It does matter.

Notice the little things.

Say something.

Say anything.

Compliments facilitate tension reduction.

Daily gestures of gratuitous kindness are the foundation upon which successful long-term relationships are based.

THE DIRTY HALF DOZEN

Rule One:
DON'T KEEP THE ROMANCE ALIVE.

Rule Two:
DON'T FIGHT FAIR.

Rule Three:
DON'T TALK ABOUT EVERYTHING.

Rule Four:
DON'T ALWAYS TELL THE TRUTH.

Rule Five:
DON'T LET GO OF THE MONEY.

Rule Six:
DON'T WORRY ABOUT WHAT YOU THINK IS IMPORTANT.

THE AUTHOR

William Nagler, M.D., is one of the nation's leading psychiatric authorities on interpersonal skills and effective relationship communication. Dr. Nagler is a graduate of the University of Michigan and the University of California and did a fellowship at Harvard. A popular professional speaker, he has appeared on *The Joan Rivers Show*, *Larry King Live*, *Sally Jessy Raphael*, and hundreds of other radio and television shows across the country. Dr. Nagler is a Diplomate of the American Board of Psychiatry and Neurology and a Diplomate of the American Board of Weight Reduction Medicine.